W9-BYJ-729

MAR - - 2014

SEA TURTLES

▲ SAMANTHA BELL

CHERRY LAKE
Publishing

Published in the United States of America by Cherry Lake Publishing
Ann Arbor, Michigan
www.cherrylakepublishing.com

Consultants: Dominique A. Didier, PhD, Associate Professor, Department of Biology, Millersville University;
Marla Conn, ReadAbility, Inc.
Book design: Sleeping Bear Press

Photo Credits: ©Soren Egeberg Photography/Shutterstock Images, cover, 1; ©Willyam Bradberry/Shutterstock Images,
5; ©Transnirvana/Dreamstime.com, 6; ©ACEgan/Shutterstock Images, 9; ©Dorling Kindersley RF/Thinkstock, 10;
©NER Sea Turtle Stranding Network/http://www.flickr.com/CC-BY-2.0, 11; ©Isabelle Kuehn/Shutterstock Images, 13;
©Joe Quinn/Shutterstock Images, 15; ©Mark Doherty/Dreamstime.com, 16; ©Matt Jeppson/Shutterstock Images, 19;
©David Evison/Shutterstock Images, 20; ©JodiJacobson/iStockphoto, 23; ©FamVeld/Shutterstock Images, 25; ©NOAA
PIFSC/http://www.flickr.com/CC-BY-2.0, 27; ©David Patte/U.S. Fish and Wildlife Service/http://www.flickr.com/
CC-BY-2.0, 28; ©Bonnie Strawser/U.S. Fish and Wildlife Service/http://www.flickr.com/CC-BY-2.0, 29

Library of Congress Cataloging-in-Publication Data

Bell, Samantha, author.
Sea turtles / Samantha Bell.
    pages cm. — (Exploring our oceans)
    Summary: "Introduces facts about sea turtles, including physical features, habitat, life cycle, food,
and threats to these ocean creatures. Photos, captions, and keywords supplement the narrative of
this informational text"— Provided by publisher.
    Audience: 8-12.
    Audience: Grades 4 to 6.
    Includes bibliographical references and index.
    ISBN 978-1-62431-602-9 (hardcover) — ISBN 978-1-62431-614-2 (pbk.) —
ISBN 978-1-62431-626-5 (pdf) — ISBN 978-1-62431-638-8 (ebook)
    1. Sea turtles—Juvenile literature. I. Title.

    QL666.C536B45 2014
    597.92'8—dc23   2013031931

Cherry Lake Publishing would like to acknowledge the work of
The Partnership for 21st Century Skills. Please visit www.p21.org
for more information.

Printed in the United States of America
Corporate Graphics Inc.
January 2014

ABOUT THE AUTHOR

Samantha Bell is a children's writer and illustrator living in South Carolina with her husband, four
children, and lots of animals. She has illustrated a number of picture books, including some of her
own. She has also written magazine articles, stories, and poems, as well as craft, activity, and wildlife
books. She loves animals, being outdoors, and learning about all the amazing wonders of nature.

TABLE OF CONTENTS

CHAPTER 1

A TURTLE'S COMPASS

When people take trips by boat or plane, they rely on a navigator, someone to make sure they are going in the right direction. Sea turtles don't need a navigator. From the time they hatch, they know just where to go. They spend several years in the open water, then they move to feeding sites. Later they return to the same beach where they hatched to lay eggs of their own. Some will travel thousands of miles all the way across the ocean and back.

Sea turtles are solitary animals. They mostly swim alone, although they sometimes nest together. Their shape and strong front flippers help them go long distances and dive deep into the ocean. They come up for air every few minutes, though some dives can last 30 minutes or more. When they are resting, sea turtles can stay underwater for several hours.

Fifth-grade students in South Carolina chose the loggerhead sea turtle as their state's reptile in 1988.

Flatbacks breed and nest only in Australia.

There are seven species of sea turtles, the leatherback, flatback, hawksbill, olive ridley, Kemp's ridley, loggerhead, and green sea turtle. They can be found all over the world, and six of them can be found around the United States. The flatback sea turtle, however, lives only near the **continental shelf** of northern Australia.

Sea turtles are marine reptiles, so they are cold-blooded. They keep their body temperature the same as their surroundings. Because of this, most sea turtles prefer tropical and **temperate** waters. However, leatherbacks and loggerheads have been seen as far north as Canada and northern Europe. Green sea turtles are found in warm coastal waters around the world, building their nests in more than 80 different countries.

GO DEEPER

WHAT OTHER REPTILES LIVE IN THE OCEAN?
WHERE DO YOU THINK YOU WOULD FIND THEM?

CHAPTER 2

ALL COLORS AND SIZES

Like other turtles, the sea turtle's shell helps protect its soft body from predators. But unlike other turtles, the sea turtle can't pull its head or flippers inside. The shell has two parts, the **carapace** and the **plastron**. The carapace is made up of many bones covered by scales called **scutes**. The number and design of the scutes on the shell help scientists identify the species. The leatherback has scutes only as a hatchling. As the leatherback grows, it sheds the scutes. Its shell is covered with thick, leathery skin.

The leatherback dives deeper than any other sea turtle.

BODY DIAGRAM

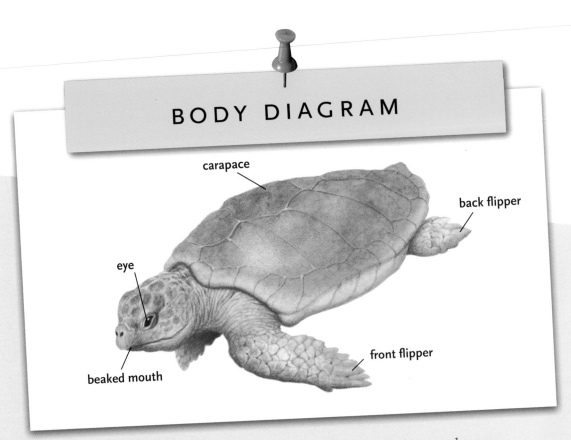

carapace

back flipper

eye

front flipper

beaked mouth

Loggerhead turtles use a plate in their beak-like mouth to crush prey.
Turtles are the only group of reptiles that don't have teeth.

The color of the sea turtle's shell depends on the species. Kemp's ridleys are grayish green, and olive ridleys are olive green. Loggerhead sea turtles are reddish brown. Green sea turtles are usually gray, black, or brown. These turtles actually get their name from the color of the body fat under their skin. Hawksbills have a beautiful brown shell with streaks of orange and red.

Sea turtles range in size from the small ridley turtles to the huge leatherbacks. Olive and Kemp's ridleys have wide, round shells that are about 2 feet (0.6 m) long. They weigh between 85 and 100 pounds (39 and 45 kg). Leatherbacks are the largest, usually growing to between 4 and 6 feet (1.2 and 1.8 m) long. Some have even been reported at 8 feet (2.4 m) long! Many weigh up to 1,500 pounds (680 kg), with the largest leatherback recorded at 2,000 pounds (907 kg). That's as heavy as a small car!

The Kemp's ridley is named after Richard M. Kemp, a fisherman and naturalist from Key West, Florida.

Whatever their size, all sea turtles seem to glide effortlessly through the water. To move forward, they flap their front flippers, which are shaped like airplane wings, up and down. They use their shorter rear flippers for steering.

Sea turtles use their senses to navigate through the ocean. They can see well underwater, and even see in color. They have a good sense of smell, detecting odors by pumping water in and out of their nostrils. Their very sensitive ears are under the scaly skin that covers their heads, and they can pick up on sounds that humans cannot hear. If a hatchling can't see the way to the ocean, it will use the sound of the surf to find it.

Sea turtles also have a magnetic sense used to help them find their way. It works with the earth's **magnetic field**, much like the compass a sailor uses. Even as hatchlings, the turtles can detect changes in the magnetic field.

This sea turtle swims gracefully near coral reefs.

LOOK AGAIN

LOOK AT THIS IMAGE CLOSELY. AFTER READING THE DESCRIPTIONS OF DIFFERENT SEA TURTLES CAN YOU DETERMINE WHICH ONE THIS IS?

WHAT'S ON THE MENU?

Adult sea turtles have favorite coastal feeding sites. Throughout their lives, they migrate between these feeding areas and the nesting beaches. Sea turtles don't have teeth, but they do have strong mouths or beaks. They use these to eat a variety of foods.

Some sea turtle species are **carnivorous**, eating other marine animals. Loggerheads dine on clams, crabs, shrimp, sea urchins, sponges, octopuses, squid, and fish. As they migrate across the open seas, they will also add jellyfish and flying fish to their diet. Kemp's

The loggerhead has strong, large jaws used to crush hard-shelled prey.

ridley sea turtles mostly eat crabs, though they will also catch fish, lobster, **mollusks**, shrimp, and jellyfish. Flatbacks also feed on marine **invertebrates**.

Olive ridleys are **omnivorous**, adding algae to their diet. Leatherbacks also eat both plants and animals, including seaweed, fish, mollusks, and **crustaceans**. However, most of their diet is made up of jellyfish. Leatherbacks have spines in their throats that point downward. The turtles swallow the jellyfish, and the spines keep the jellyfish from coming back up.

Green sea turtles eat sea grass and algae. This is believed to give them greenish-colored fat.

Hawksbill sea turtles are named for their narrow, pointed beaks. Their favorite foods are sponges. The beaks help the turtles pull the sponges from the reefs. Some of the sponges are poisonous, but that doesn't bother these turtles. Hawksbills also eat sea grasses, algae, fish, barnacles, and sea urchins.

Unlike the other species, green sea turtles are mostly **herbivores**. They feed on algae and sea grass. Baby green sea turtles are the exception. They eat not only grasses but also aquatic insects, crustaceans, and worms. The green sea turtle's jaw is **serrated** like a knife. This makes the sea grass easier to chew.

16

Turtles often dive as they search for food, and some can go to extreme depths. Loggerheads can dive down 750 feet (228.6 m). Olive ridleys have been known to dive as deep as 950 feet (289.5 m). Leatherbacks, however, go even farther. They've been known to go more than 3,900 feet (1,188.7 m) deep!

The food that sea turtles eat contains a lot of salt. Special salt glands in their heads remove extra salt from their bodies. The turtles look like they are crying, but their "tears" are actually necessary for survival.

THINK ABOUT IT

CONSIDER THE FOODS YOU'VE EATEN DURING THE LAST WEEK. ARE YOU CARNIVOROUS, OMNIVOROUS, OR HERBIVOROUS?

BABIES ON THEIR OWN

All female sea turtles lay eggs. A mother turtle will make her way back to the same beach where she hatched many years before. There she will dig a nest, lay her clutch of eggs, and go back to the ocean. Unlike other animals, she doesn't care for her young.

Depending on the species, sea turtles lay eggs from March to September. Most will crawl up from the ocean at night, although the Kemp's ridleys often nest during the day. The female turtle uses her flippers to get on the beach. If she can't find a good nesting place or is disturbed, she will go back into the ocean. About half of the nesting attempts end in a false crawl. This means the turtle wasn't able to lay her eggs.

After laying her eggs, the female turtle will cover them.

Turtles use their flippers for swimming and for digging and covering nests.

If the turtle does select a site, she will dig the nest with her back flippers. The sea turtle will lay 80 to 100 or more round, white, leathery eggs. The eggs of most sea turtles are close to the size of a Ping-Pong ball. A leatherback's eggs are larger, about the size of a racquetball. After the female lays the last egg, she fills in the nest with sand and packs it down. Then she flings more sand over the pit to hide it. Soon she drags herself back to the ocean and swims away. Some turtles may return five or six additional times to lay more eggs, each time in a new nest.

When the nesting season is over, the female will make her way back to the feeding sites. She will stay there for the next two to three years. When it's time to nest again, she'll return to the same beach.

Meanwhile, the sun heats up the sand, which **incubates** the eggs. If a certain temperature is reached, half of the turtles will be males and half will be females. However, if the sand is warmer, they will all be females. If the sand is cooler, they will all be males.

After 50 to 60 days, the eggs hatch. The babies work together to climb out of the nest. When they are near the surface, the ones on the top feel the temperature of the sand. If it's warm, they wait until the sand cools down. Cool sand means that it's nighttime. The baby turtles are less likely to be seen by predators or become overheated. Breaking through the sand, the hatchlings hurry to the ocean. To find their way, they use cues like the natural light of the horizon. They also follow the slope of the beach and the sound of the surf.

Once in the water, the 1.5-inch (3.8 cm) hatchlings swim to the open sea. There they will grow and develop on their own. Scientists call this period the "lost years" because it is so difficult to find and study the juvenile turtles. After several more years, the turtles move on to their feeding sites. Ocean currents carry some of the turtles to the other side of the world. Loggerheads that hatched in the United States have turned up years later in the Mediterranean Sea. Others born in Japan have been found feeding in Mexico.

Sea turtles will typically spend more than 10 years at sea before returning to the beaches where they hatched. There they find mates, and the females trudge onto the sand to lay eggs.

Hundreds of sea turtles will hatch at once, and they must make their way quickly to the sea.

LOOK AGAIN

LOOK AT THIS IMAGE CLOSELY. WHAT IS SOMETHING THAT SURPRISES YOU ABOUT WHAT YOU SEE?

CHAPTER 5

PREDATORS AND THREATS

Scientists are unsure how long sea turtles live in the wild. Some might live 60, 80, or 100 years, or even more. And out of every 1,000 hatchlings, only one will make it all the way to adulthood.

The eggs are a favorite food of raccoons, skunks, foxes, coyotes, lizards, snakes, and beetles. If the eggs do hatch, the little turtles must make it past more predators, including seagulls and ghost crabs.

Once hatchlings reach the water, they swim nonstop into deeper water to escape predators near the shore. Out at sea, fish and birds will try to catch them. Grown turtles are a favorite food of sharks.

These baby turtles have reached the shore, having escaped some predators.

Even with these dangerous predators, the biggest threat to the turtles comes from humans. When people build businesses and houses close to shore, they change the natural nesting sites of the turtles. If the turtles are able to nest, the hatchlings have other problems. The small turtles use the light of the night sky to guide them. Other lights from houses, hotels, and cars lead them in the wrong direction.

Fishermen pose another threat. They don't want the turtles, but they accidently hook them or catch them in their nets. Loggerheads and leatherbacks migrating across the ocean can get caught on longline hooks. Other turtles can get caught in nets that are dragged through the water. Fishermen looking for shrimp scoop up not only the shrimp, but everything else as well. Devices have been installed on nets to prevent sea turtles from getting caught. Sadly, some turtles still get caught in the nets and drown.

Humans using nets like this one can accidently catch sea turtles.

LOOK AGAIN

LOOK CLOSELY AT THIS PHOTO. WHAT STANDS OUT TO YOU? HOW
WOULD YOU DESCRIBE THIS PHOTO TO A FRIEND OR CLASSMATE?

These green sea turtles live at a national wildlife refuge in Hawaii.

Pollution and trash thrown in the ocean can harm the sea turtles. Plastic bags in the water look a lot like jellyfish to a turtle. The turtles eat the bags and die. Oil spills also cause problems. The turtles can't breathe easily or "cry" away the extra salt.

All seven sea turtle species are listed as threatened or **endangered**. The International Union for Conservation of Nature classifies the Kemp's ridley, leatherback, and hawksbill as Critically Endangered on its Red List of Threatened Species. This means that populations have an extremely high risk of becoming extinct.

National laws and international treaties have been created to protect sea turtles. Some nesting beaches have been turned into wildlife preserves. People who live near nesting beaches turn off their lights during the nesting season. This helps hatchlings find their way to the sea. Changes made to fishing gear have allowed turtles to escape if caught by accident. By recognizing the problems and working together, we can find ways to help the sea turtles survive.

Sometimes sea turtle nests are moved by experts to keep the delicate eggs safe.

THINK ABOUT IT

- What is the most interesting fact you learned about sea turtles? What else would you like to know? Find another source of information about these reptiles. How does it compare to what you have already learned?

- Did this book change your view of sea turtles? If so, how?

- Review chapter 4. What is the main idea? Choose two or three details that support the main idea.

- In chapter 5 you learned all seven species of sea turtles are threatened or endangered. Find a Web site with information about oil spills and their impact on wildlife.

LEARN MORE

FURTHER READING

Gibbons, Gail. *Sea Turtles*. New York: Holiday House, 1995.

Kalman, Bobbie. *Endangered Sea Turtles*. New York: Crabtree Publishing, 2004.

Lasky, Kathryn. *Interrupted Journey: Saving Endangered Sea Turtles*. Cambridge, MA: Candlewick Press, 2001.

Rathmell, Donna. *Carolina's Story: Sea Turtles Get Sick Too!* Mt. Pleasant, SC: Sylvan Dell Publishing, 2005.

WEB SITES

The Georgia Sea Turtle Center—GSTC Kids: Scute's Spot
www.georgiaseaturtlecenter.org/kids-spot
Explore the wonderful world of sea turtles.

National Geographic Kids—Reptiles: Baby Loggerhead Turtles
http://video.nationalgeographic.com/video/kids/animals-pets-kids/reptiles-kids/turtle-loggerhead-kids
Watch a video of baby loggerheads as they make their way from the sand to sea.

NOAA's National Marine Fisheries Service—The Kid's Times: Loggerhead Sea Turtle
www.nmfs.noaa.gov/pr/pdfs/education/kids_times_turtle_loggerhead.pdf
Read a newsletter with articles devoted to the loggerhead.

GLOSSARY

carapace (KEHR-uh-pehss) the top shell of a turtle

carnivorous (kahr-NIV-uh-russ) eating other animals

continental shelf (kahn-tuh-NEN-tuhl SHELF) area of the seafloor near a coastline

crustaceans (kruh-STAY-shuhnz) a sea creature that has an outer skeleton including lobsters, crabs, shrimp, barnacles, and water fleas

endangered (en-DAYN-jurd) at risk of becoming extinct or of dying out

herbivores (HUR-buh-vorz) animals that eat only plants

incubates (ING-kyu-bayts) to keep eggs warm so they will develop

invertebrates (in-VUR-tuh-brits) animals without a backbone

magnetic field (mag-NEH-tik FEELD) a region where a magnetic force is detectable

mollusks (MAH-luhsks) soft-bodied animals that have no backbones and are often enclosed in shells

omnivorous (om-NIH-vuh-russ) eating both plants and animals

plastron (PLASS-trahn) the bottom shell of a turtle

scutes (SKYOOTS) scales that form the shell of most species of sea turtles

serrated (SEHR-ayt-id) having a jagged edge, like a saw

temperate (TEM-pur-it) mild temperatures

INDEX

[21ST CENTURY SKILLS LIBRARY]